ISBN-13: 978-1546850588

ISBN-10: 1546850589

DEDICATION

Asia - Europe new order

"Along the way" to write a vision of the global economic development blueprint, revealing the future of the new world order. "Along the way" to continue the ancient Silk Road to innovate the spirit of international trade exchange model for the 21st century to provide a shared growth, promote sustainable development of the forward program.

"The road along the way" means the "Silk Road Economic Belt" on the land and the "21st Century Maritime Silk Road" across the sea, across the Eurasian continent, covering more than 60 countries and regions in Southeast Asia, South Asia, Central Asia, West Asia and the Middle East , The current GDP accounted for three percent of the world, trade in goods accounted for more than three percent of the global total.

By 2050, the Gross Global Product (GDP) growth is expected to come from "one country" and the region, with 3 billion more among them.

CONTENTS

内容

ACKNOWLEDGMENTS

The Belt and Road Initiative is a systematic project, which should be jointly built through consultation to meet the interests of all, and efforts should be made to integrate the development strategies of the countries along the Belt and Road. The Chinese government has drafted and published the Vision and Actions on Jointly Building Silk Road Economic Belt and 21st-Century Maritime Silk Road to promote the implementation of the Initiative, instill vigor and vitality into the ancient Silk Road, connect Asian, European and African countries more closely and promote mutually beneficial cooperation to a new high and in new forms.

1 **BACKGROUND**

Asia - Europe new order

"Along the way" to write a vision of the global economic development blueprint, revealing the future of the new world order. "Along the way" to continue the ancient Silk Road to innovate the spirit of international trade exchange model for the 21st century to provide a shared growth, promote sustainable development of the forward program.

"The road along the way" means the "Silk Road Economic Belt" on the land and the "21st Century Maritime Silk Road" across the sea, across the Eurasian continent, covering more than 60 countries and regions in Southeast Asia, South Asia, Central Asia, West Asia and the Middle East , The current GDP accounted for three percent of the world, trade in goods accounted for more than three percent of the global total.

By 2050, the Gross Global Product (GDP) growth is expected to come from "one country" and the region, with 3 billion more among them.

Exhibit 3: Trans-Asian railway network

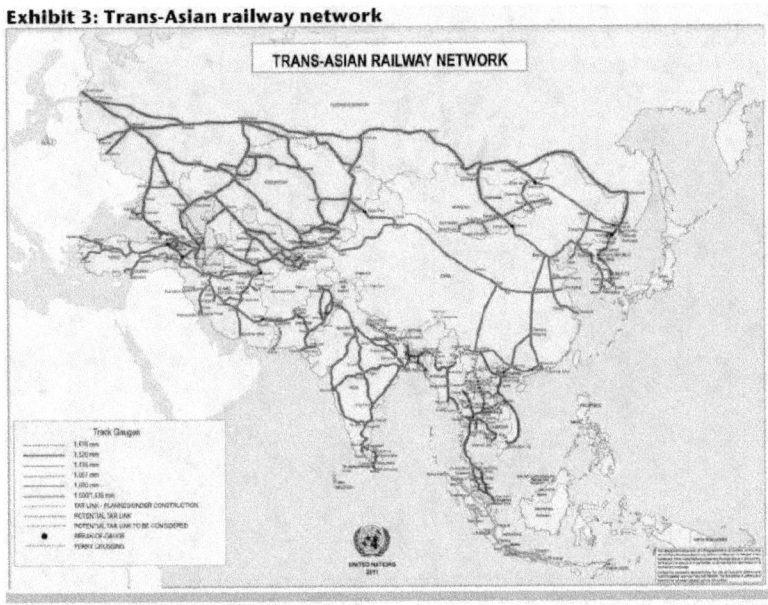

Source: United Nations, Jefferies

Turn on new business opportunities The "One Way" is designed to promote the deep integration of the market and to strengthen the links between different economies, injecting momentum into the flow of funds, goods and services between Asia and the rest of the world. "Take all the way" to bring new opportunities for global businesses, so that multinational companies and even SMEs to develop new markets, and with the Chinese mainland, ASEAN, the Middle East, Central and Eastern Europe and other places to expand business opportunities. While the investment in emerging economies and trade activities increased, is bound to accelerate the overall development of society, so that the parties benefit.

The Belt and Road Initiative: Six Economic Corridors Spanning Asia, Europe and Africa

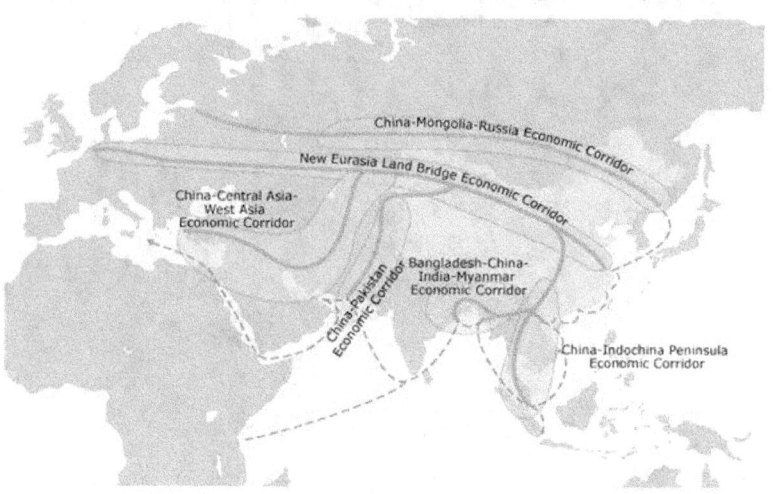

2 PRINCIPLES

"One way along the way" will be through five to Asia and Africa through the continent. Among them, the Silk Road economic belt has a clear focus (1) China by Central Asia, Russia
To Europe; (2) China through Central Asia, West Asia to the Middle East, the Mediterranean; (3) China to Southeast Asia, South Asia, the Indian Ocean. While the 21st century sea silk (4) from the Chinese coastal ports across the South China Sea to the Indian Ocean, extending to Europe; and (5) from the Chinese coastal ports to the South China Sea to South Pacific foreign.
According to the above five trends, "along the way" construction will rely on the international traffic corridor to the central city along the key and the port as a node, into a
To promote the cooperation, to create a new Eurasian Continental Bridge, China and Mongolia, China - Central Asia - West Asia, China - Indochina Peninsula, China and Pakistan and India
Six international economic corridors

FROM INITIATIVE TO REALITY

- China unveiled on March 28 the principles, framework, and cooperation priorities and mechanisms in its Belt and Road Initiative in a bid to enhance regional connectivity and embrace a brighter future together.

- The action plan, jointly released by the National Development and Reform Commission, Ministry of Foreign Affairs and Ministry of Commerce, offered insight in the China-initiated program's vision and endeavors.

- Click for the major events in the development of China's Belt and Road Initiative so far.

(1) New Eurasian Continental Bridge Economic Corridor
The new Eurasian Continental Bridge, also known as "the second Eurasian Continental Bridge", is from China's Jiangsu Lianyungang by Xinjiang Alashankou to the Netherlands Rotterdam's international iron
Road traffic trunk. Domestic by the Longhai Railway and Lan Xin Railway, through China's eastern, central and western provinces and cities. After leaving the country by Kazakh, Russia
Sri Lanka, Poland to the European multinational coastal ports. Relying on the new Eurasian Continental Bridge, China has now opened from Chongqing to Germany Duisburg
Of the "Chongqing new European" international freight class, from Wuhan to the Czech Republic Merlin Karpdudu than the "Han Xin Europe" cargo train, from Chengdu to Poland
And the "Zheng Xin Europe" freight train from Zhengzhou to Hamburg, Germany, to carry out iron and steel transport, and promised to transport along the way
Lose is "a declaration, a check, a release."

3FRAMEWORK

(2) Sino-Russian economic corridor China and Mongolia, the three countries connected to each other has long been in the inter-city trade, border areas of cooperation in a different degree of economic exchanges and cooperation For. In September 2014, the heads of the three countries of China, Russia and Mongolia met for the first time during the meeting of the Shanghai Cooperation Organization Dusanbe, agreed in China, Russia, Russia and Mongolia on the basis of bilateral cooperation to carry out tripartite cooperation, clear the tripartite cooperation in the principles, direction and focus areas. The three heads of state also agreed to China "Silk Road Economic Zone" construction with Russia across the Eurasian railway transformation, Mongolia "grassland road" initiative docking cooperation, strengthen the railway, Roads and other interconnection construction, promote customs clearance and transport facilitation, and promote transit transport cooperation, to create the Russian-Russian economic corridor. July 2015 Sino-Russian Mongolian heads of state in Russia Ufa for the second meeting, approved the "People's Republic of China, the Russian Federation, Mongolia, the development of tripartite For the mid-term road map. "

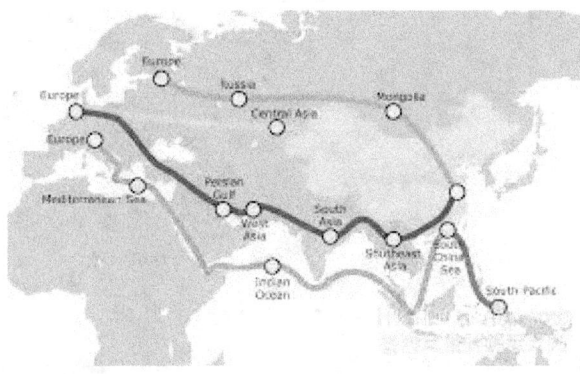

(3) China - Central Asia - West Asia Economic Corridor China - Central Asia - West Asia Economic Corridor from Xinjiang, via the Alashankou exit connecting Central Asia and West Asia Railway network to reach the Mediterranean coast and Allah The peninsula, mainly involved in the five Central Asian countries (Kazakhstan, Kyrgyzstan, Tajikistan, Uzbekistan, Turkmenistan), and West Asia, Iran, Turkey and other countries. The "China-Central Asia Economic Cooperation Zone", which was held in Shandong in June 2015, will be incorporated into China and the five countries of Central Asia. Joint Declaration of Political Documents. Previously, China has signed with Tajik, Kazak, Kyrgyzstan has jointly built the Silk Road economic belt with bilateral Cooperation agreement, and also signed with Uzbekistan to build "Silk Road Economic Zone" cooperation documents, will further deepen and expand the two countries in trade Easy, investment, finance and transportation and other fields of mutually beneficial cooperation. The national development strategies of the five Central Asian countries, including the "bright road" of Kazakhstan, Tajik "energy transport food" three Xingguo strategy, Turkmenistan "strong and happy times" and so on with the Silk Road economic zone construction formed a contract Point together.

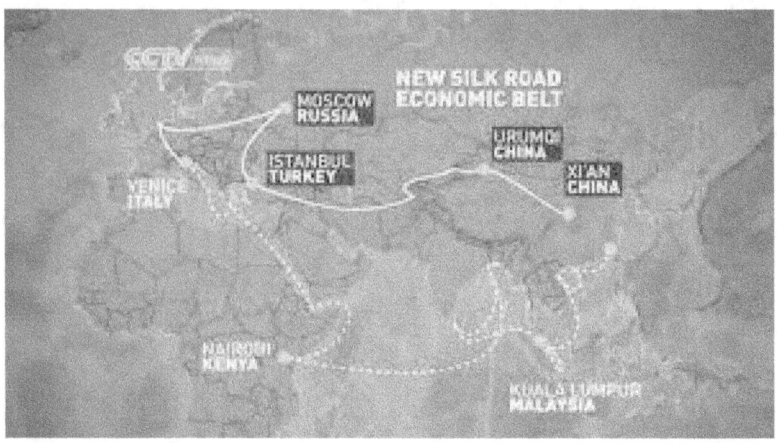

(4) China - Zhongnan Peninsula Economic Corridor Chinese Premier Li Keqiang deepened in December 2014 when he attended the fifth meeting of leaders of the Greater Mekong Subregion Economic Cooperation in Bangkok The country has made three suggestions on the relations with the five countries of the Indochina Peninsula, including (1) jointly planning and building all-round transportation network and industrial cooperation projects (2) to build a new model of financing cooperation, and (3) to promote sustainable and coordinated economic and social development. At present, the Greater Mekong Basin countries are In the construction of things through, connecting the north and south of the nine cross-border roads, some of which have been completed, for example, Guangxi has built a gateway to the friendship and the East Xingkou highway. In addition, Guangxi has also opened Nanning to Hanoi international train and connecting other major cities in Southeast Asia flights.

4 COOPERATION PRIORITIES

China-Pakistan Economic Corridor
China and Pakistan Economic Corridor in May 2013, when
Premier Li Keqiang visited Pakistan, the goal is to build a north
from Xinjiang Kashi, south to Guadal
Seoul's economic arteries. At present, the two governments have
initially formulated the construction of Xinjiang Kashi City to
Pakistan southwest port Gwadar port roads, railways,
Long - term Planning of Oil and Gas Pipeline and Cable - covered
Channel. In accordance with the joint sound of China and Pakistan
in Islamabad in April 2015
Ming, China and Pakistan will actively promote the modernization
of the Karakoram Highway Phase II (Tecot to Zhaowei section),
Gwadar Port East Bay Expressway, the new country
International Airport, Karachi to Lahore Highway (Moulantan to
Sukul section), Lahore Rail Transit Orange Line, Haier-Luba
Economic Zone,
Pakistan cross-border cable and other key cooperation projects.

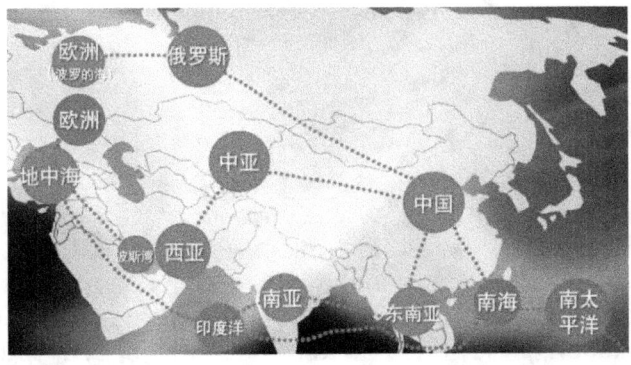

(6) Mengzhong India and Burma economic corridor In May 2013, during the visit to India, China and India jointly initiated the construction of the Bangladesh-India-Burma-Burma economic corridor. December 2013, Mengzhong India and Burma economic corridor The first meeting of the Joint Working Group was held in Kunming, and representatives of the four governments expressed their views on the development prospects of economic corridors, priority areas of cooperation and mechanisms And to reach a broad consensus on specific areas such as transportation infrastructure, investment and trade circulation, cultural exchange and so on. Parties sign The establishment of the minutes of the meeting and the Bangladesh-India-India Economic Corridor joint research program, formally established the four governments to promote cooperation between Bangladesh and India and India mechanism.

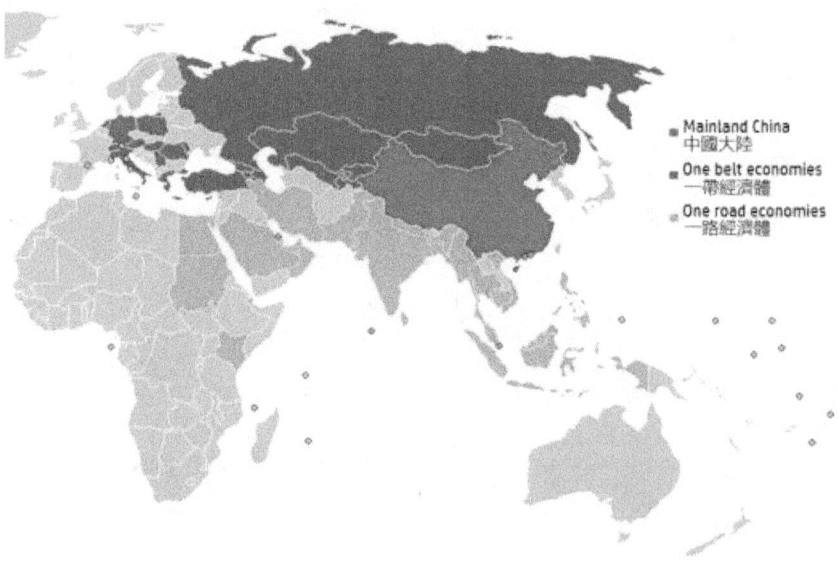

"One way all the way" will be "five links", that is, policy communication, facilities, Unicom, trade flow, financial intermediation, the same as the main content. Policy communication is through the countries through the equal consultation, jointly develop to promote national or regional cooperation between the development planning and measures, To provide policy support for pragmatic cooperation and large-scale project implementation. Infrastructure interconnection is a priority area for "building all the way". Will give priority to open the international backbone of the lack of traffic links and bottlenecks, to promote the construction of port infrastructure, smooth land and water transport channels. Promote along the national railway, road, aviation, telecommunications, oil and gas pipelines, Ports and other infrastructure to achieve interoperability, and gradually formed to connect the Asian region and Asia-Africa and Africa between the infrastructure network.

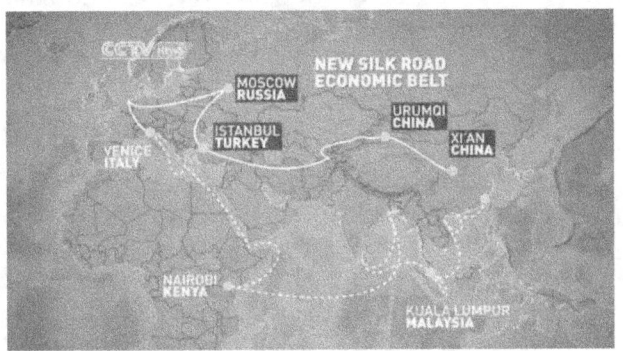

Trade flow, research to solve the problem of investment and trade facilitation, reduce trade and investment barriers, reduce trade and investment costs, promote regional economy Integration. Broaden the scope of trade, investment to promote trade development, and strengthen cooperation with the relevant countries in the industrial chain. Capital financing, to strengthen monetary policy coordination, to expand the national trade and investment in the local currency settlement and currency exchange, deepen the bilateral financial Cooperation, the construction of regional development of financial institutions, strengthen financial risk supervision and cooperation, through regional arrangements to enhance the ability to resist financial risks. In the field of cultural exchanges, it will promote dialogue and exchange between different civilizations, strengthen friendly exchanges between peoples, enhance mutual understanding and traditional friendship To lay the foundation of public opinion and social basis for regional cooperation.

Cooperation mechanism
"Build all the way" construction We will persist in discussing, building and sharing the principle, and actively using the existing double multilateral cooperation mechanism to promote the national development strategy
Of the docking. To promote the signing of a memorandum of cooperation or cooperation planning, the construction of a number of bilateral cooperation demonstration. Establish and improve the bilateral joint working mechanism,
To study the implementation of the "one way around" the implementation of the program, the road map.

Silk Road Fund
Silk Road funds are $ 40 billion in funds, will be "along the way" along the infrastructure construction, resource development, industry and financial cooperation
And other related projects to provide investment and financing support. Silk Road Fund Co., Ltd. was established in December 2014, the founding shareholders, including China's national foreign exchange
Bureau of China Investment Co., Ltd., China Export-Import Bank and China National Development Bank. Funds will comply with market rules and international finance
Order and welcomes the participation of domestic and overseas investors, such as the Central African Development Fund and the Asian Infrastructure Investment Bank.

Silk Road Fund's first capital of 10 billion US dollars. On May 14, 2017, Chinese President Xi Jinping attended the "International Cooperation"
Summit Forum opening ceremony delivered a keynote speech, announced that the new funds will be added to the Silk Road Fund 100 billion yuan.

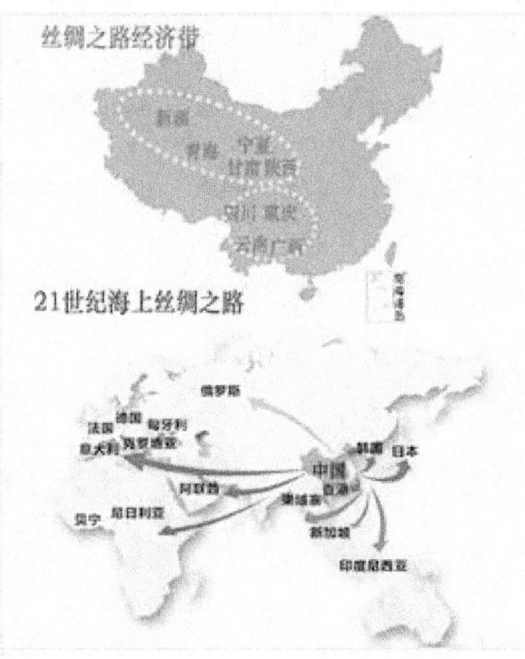

The Asian Infrastructure Investment Bank is a newly established multilateral development bank that works with existing multilateral development banks and works with each other.
Asia's financing needs for infrastructure construction. ADB will focus on infrastructure development and other productive sectors in Asia, including energy and electricity
Forces, transport and telecommunications, rural infrastructure and agricultural development, water supply and sanitation, environmental protection, urban development and logistics.
In December 2015, all of the 57 Asian Investment Bank Founding Member States have signed the Asian Infrastructure Investment Bank Agreement, which includes Australia

Asia, Austria, Azerbaijan, Bangladesh, Brazil, Brunei, Cambodia, China, Denmark, Egypt, Finland, France, Georgia, Germany, Iceland, India, Indonesia, Iran, Israel, Italy, Jordan, Kazakhstan, South Korea, Kyrgyzstan, Kuwait, Laos, Luxembourg, Malaysia, Maldives, Malta, Mongolia, Myanmar, Nepal, the Netherlands, New Zealand, Norway, Oman, Pakistan Tanzania, Poland, Portugal, Qatar, Russia, Saudi Arabia, Singapore, South Africa, Spain, Sri Lanka, Switzerland Code, Switzerland, Tajikistan, Thailand, Turkey, UAE, United Kingdom, Uzbekistan and Vietnam. As of May 13, 2017, the Asian Investment Bank
There are 77 full members / approved members (including Hong Kong).

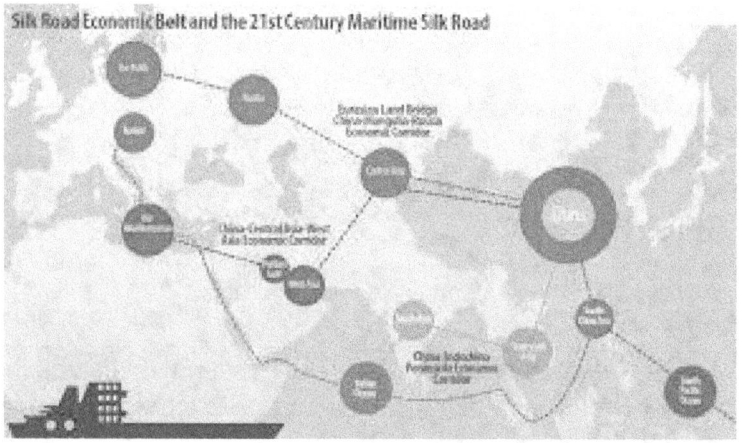

We should continue to encourage the constructive role of the international forums and exhibitions at regional and subregional levels hosted by countries along the Belt and Road, as well as such platforms as Boao Forum for Asia, China-ASEAN Expo, China-Eurasia Expo, Euro-Asia Economic Forum, China International Fair for Investment and Trade, China-South Asia Expo, China-Arab States Expo, Western China International Fair, China-Russia Expo, and Qianhai Cooperation Forum. We should support the local authorities and general public of countries along the Belt and Road to explore the historical and cultural heritage of the Belt and Road, jointly hold investment, trade and cultural exchange activities, and ensure the success of the Silk Road (Dunhuang) International Culture Expo, Silk Road International Film Festival and Silk Road International Book Fair. We propose to set up an international summit forum on the Belt and Road Initiative.

5 CHINA'S REGIONS IN PURSUING OPENING-UP

In advancing the Belt and Road Initiative, China will fully leverage the comparative advantages of its various regions, adopt a proactive strategy of further opening-up, strengthen interaction and cooperation among the eastern, western and central regions, and comprehensively improve the openness of the Chinese economy.

Northwestern and northeastern regions. We should make good use of Xinjiang's geographic advantages and its role as a window of westward opening-up to deepen communication and cooperation with Central, South and West Asian countries, make it a key transportation, trade, logistics, culture, science and education center, and a core area on the Silk Road Economic Belt. We should give full scope to the economic and cultural strengths of Shaanxi and Gansu provinces and the ethnic and cultural advantages of the Ningxia Hui autonomous region and Qinghai province, build Xi'an into a new focus of reform and opening-up in China's interior, speed up the development and opening-up of cities such as Lanzhou and Xining, and advance the building of the Ningxia Inland Opening-up Pilot Economic Zone with the goal of creating strategic channels, trade and logistics hubs and key bases for industrial and cultural exchanges opening to Central, South and West Asian countries. We should give full play to Inner Mongolia's proximity to Mongolia and Russia, improve the railway links connecting Heilongjiang province with Russia and the regional railway network, strengthen cooperation between China's Heilongjiang, Jilin and Liaoning provinces and Russia's Far East region on sea-land multimodal transport, and advance the construction of an Eurasian high-speed transport corridor linking Beijing and Moscow with the goal of building key windows opening to the north.

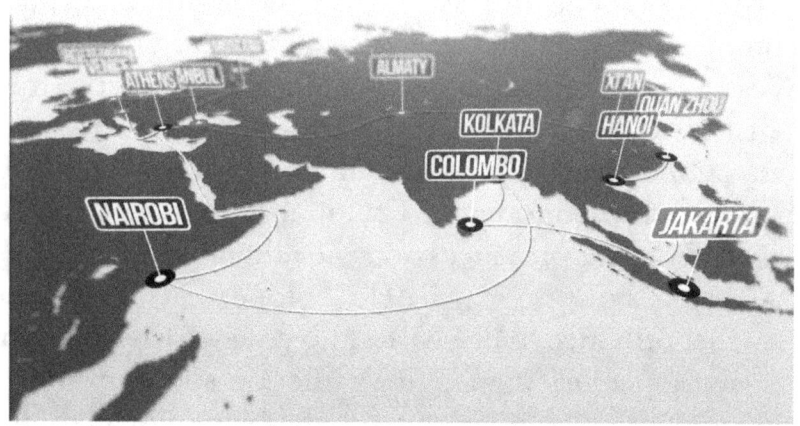

Southwestern region. We should give full play to the unique advantage of Guangxi Zhuang autonomous region as a neighbor of ASEAN countries, speed up the opening-up and development of the Beibu Gulf Economic Zone and the Pearl River-Xijiang Economic Zone, build an international corridor opening to the ASEAN region, create new strategic anchors for the opening-up and development of the southwest and mid-south regions of China, and form an important gateway connecting the Silk Road Economic Belt and the 21st-Century Maritime Silk Road. We should make good use of the geographic advantage of Yunnan province, advance the construction of an international transport corridor connecting China with neighboring countries, develop a new highlight of economic cooperation in the Greater Mekong Subregion, and make the region a pivot of China's opening-up to South and Southeast Asia. We should promote the border trade and tourism and culture cooperation between Tibet autonomous region and neighboring countries such as Nepal.

Coastal regions, and Hong Kong, Macao and Taiwan.

We should leverage the strengths of the Yangtze River Delta, Pearl River Delta, west coast of the Taiwan Straits, Bohai Rim, and other areas with economic zones boasting a high level of openness, robust economic strengths and strong catalytic role, speed up the development of the China (Shanghai) Pilot Free Trade Zone, and support Fujian province in becoming a core area of the 21st-Century Maritime Silk Road. We should give full scope to the role of Qianhai (Shenzhen), Nansha (Guangzhou), Hengqin (Zhuhai) and Pingtan (Fujian) in opening-up and cooperation, deepen their cooperation with Hong Kong, Macao and Taiwan, and help to build the Guangdong-Hong Kong-Macao Big Bay Area. We should promote the development of the Zhejiang Marine Economy Development Demonstration Zone, Fujian Marine Economic Pilot Zone and Zhoushan Archipelago New Area, and further open Hainan province as an international tourism island. We should strengthen the port construction of coastal cities such as Shanghai, Tianjin, Ningbo-Zhoushan, Guangzhou, Shenzhen, Zhanjiang, Shantou, Qingdao, Yantai, Dalian, Fuzhou, Xiamen, Quanzhou, Haikou and Sanya, and strengthen the functions of international hub airports such as Shanghai and Guangzhou. We should use opening-up to motivate these areas to carry out deeper reform, create new systems and mechanisms of open economy, step up scientific and technological innovation, develop new advantages for participating in and leading international cooperation and competition, and become the pacesetter and main force in the Belt and Road Initiative, particularly the building of the 21st-Century Maritime Silk Road. We should leverage the unique role of overseas Chinese and the Hong Kong and Macao Special Administrative Regions, and encourage them to participate in and contribute to the Belt and Road

Initiative. We should also make proper arrangements for the Taiwan region to be part of this effort.

Major industrial policy programs 2016(1)	
Financial support for industrial restructuring	PBOC, NDRC, MIIT et al.
Merging the development of the manufacturing industry and the internet	State Council
Fair competition examination system	State Council
Industrial green development, 2016-2020	MIIT
Industrial technology policy, 2016-2020	MIIT
13th Five-Year Plan for domestic trade circulation	MOFCOM, NDRC, MIIT, MOF et al.
Green manufacturing	MOF, MIIT
13th Five-Year Plan for "strategic emerging industries"	State Council
International cooperation to improve China's position in global value chains	MOFCOM, NDRC, MOST, MIIT, et al.
Smart manufacturing, 2016-2020	MIIT, MOF

Inland regions. We should make use of the advantages of inland regions, including a vast landmass, rich human resources and a strong industrial foundation, focus on such key regions as the city clusters along the middle reaches of the Yangtze River, around Chengdu and Chongqing, in central Henan province, around Hohhot, Baotou, Erdos and Yulin, and around Harbin and Changchun to propel regional interaction and cooperation and industrial concentration. We should build Chongqing into an important pivot for developing and opening up the western region, and make Chengdu, Zhengzhou, Wuhan, Changsha, Nanchang and Hefei leading areas of opening-up in the inland regions. We should accelerate cooperation between regions on the upper and middle reaches of the Yangtze River and their counterparts along Russia's Volga River. We should set up coordination mechanisms in terms of railway transport and port customs clearance for the China-Europe corridor, cultivate the brand of "China-Europe freight trains," and construct a cross-border transport corridor connecting the eastern, central and western regions. We should support inland cities such as Zhengzhou and Xi'an in building airports and international land ports, strengthen customs clearance cooperation between inland ports and ports in the coastal and border regions, and launch pilot e-commerce services for cross-border trade. We should optimize the layout of special customs oversight areas, develop new models of processing trade, and deepen industrial cooperation with countries along the Belt and Road.

6.China in Action

For more than a year, the Chinese government has been actively promoting the building of the Belt and Road, enhancing communication and consultation and advancing practical cooperation with countries along the Belt and Road, and introduced a series of policies and measures for early outcomes.

High-level guidance and facilitation. President Xi Jinping and Premier Li Keqiang have visited over 20 countries, attended the Dialogue on Strengthening Connectivity Partnership and the sixth ministerial conference of the China-Arab States Cooperation Forum, and met with leaders of relevant countries to discuss bilateral relations and regional development issues. They have used these opportunities to explain the rich contents and positive implications of the Belt and Road Initiative, and their efforts have helped bring about a broad consensus on the Belt and Road Initiative.

Signing cooperation framework. China has signed MOUs of cooperation on the joint development of the Belt and Road with some countries, and on regional cooperation and border cooperation and mid-and long-term development plans for economic and trade cooperation with some neighboring countries. It has proposed outlines of regional cooperation plans with some adjacent countries.

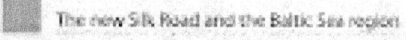

The new Silk Road and the Baltic Sea region

One Belt, One Road

by Maciej Bochno

Bill Gates, former chairman of Microsoft, is a clear supporter of a plan in mainland China and has visited China at least seven times in 2017, arguing that many people in Europe and the United States have a " The world is dangerous, so praised China's strategy along the way, so that many countries have joined, is to go out to help other countries, and admire Xi Jinping domestic poverty reduction strategy, and the global poverty alleviation progress can cause the world more stable and everyone larger Interest [19], his "Gates Foundation" is working with the Chinese Ministry of Commerce, the Ministry of Agriculture to jointly promote the sustainable development of agriculture in Africa, and agree that China's nuclear energy to solve global warming strategy is the most practical, with him Long-term view of the same, his company will be China's nuclear power company will discuss the construction of the fourth generation of nuclear power plant.

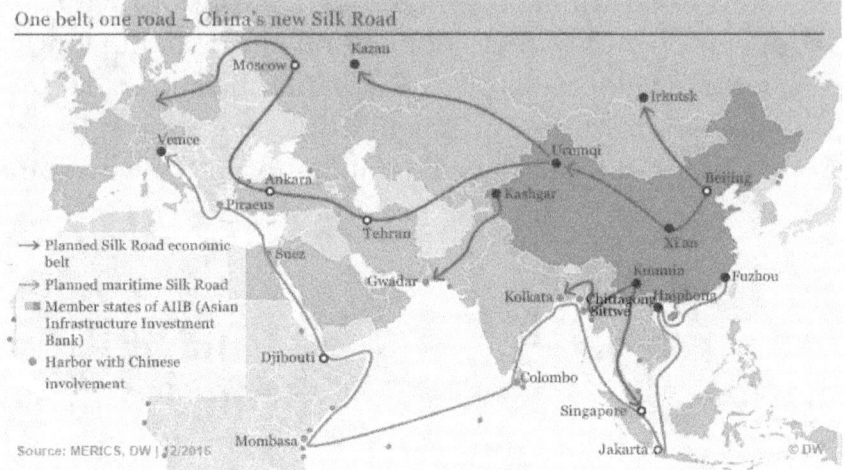

One belt, one road – China's new Silk Road

→ Planned Silk Road economic belt
→ Planned maritime Silk Road
▩ Member states of AIIB (Asian Infrastructure Investment Bank)
● Harbor with Chinese involvement

Source: MERICS, DW | 12/2015

7.Embracing a Brighter Future

Together

The Government of the People's Republic of China advocates that the way is not an entity and mechanism, but a cooperative development concept and initiative, relying on China and the countries and regions of the existing double multilateral mechanism, with the existing, effective regional cooperation platform The Aims to use the ancient "Silk Road" historical symbols, hold high the banner of peaceful development, take the initiative to develop economic and cooperative partnership with countries and regions along the common to create political mutual trust, economic integration, cultural inclusive interests of the community, the fate of the community and Responsibility Community.

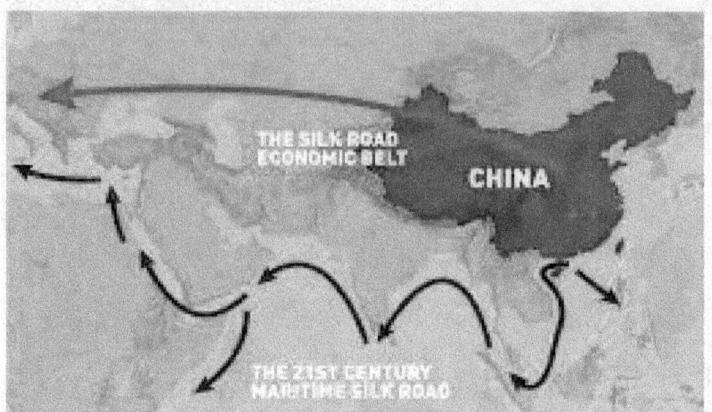

ABOUT THE AUTHOR

PENG, PO-YU

Director Of Counseling

Degree ：

1.   Information and Learning Technology，National Chiao Tung University

2.   Education Psychology and Counseling，National Hsinchu University of Education

Doctor of Philosophy:

3.   Education，National Hsinchu University of Education

e-mail:yorpong@gmail.com

Major:

E-learning Technology、English Teaching Research、Guidance & Counseling、Human Learning Behavior Research

www.ingramcontent.com/pod-product-compliance
Lightning Source LLC
Chambersburg PA
CBHW061942280526
45787CB00004B/1698